Albert L. Gihon

The Dignity and Importance of the Individual

an address to the graduating class - at the commencement of the Central

High School of Philadelphia, February 12, 1885

Albert L. Gihon

The Dignity and Importance of the Individual
*an address to the graduating class - at the commencement of the Central High
School of Philadelphia, February 12, 1885*

ISBN/EAN: 9783337837570

Printed in Europe, USA, Canada, Australia, Japan

Cover: Foto ©Andreas Hilbeck / pixelio.de

More available books at **www.hansebooks.com**

The Dignity and Importance of the Individual.

An Address to the Graduating Class, at the Commencement of the Central High School of
Philadelphia, Thursday, February 12, 1885.

By ALBERT L. GIHON, A.M., M.D.

Of the Class of February, 1850.

MEDICAL DIRECTOR UNITED STATES NAVY, PRESIDENT OF THE AMERICAN ACADEMY OF
MEDICINE, EX-PRESIDENT OF THE AMERICAN PUBLIC
HEALTH ASSOCIATION, ETC

PRINTED BY ORDER OF

BOARD OF PUBLIC EDUCATION.

Philadelphia, March 10, 1885.

At a meeting of the Board of Public Education, held on the above date, the following resolution was adopted:

Resolved, That the Committee on Office be and are hereby authorized to have not less than five thousand copies printed of the Master's Address on Health, delivered by Albert L. Gihon, A. M., M. D., Medical Director United States Navy, at the Boys' Central High School Commencement, on Thursday, February 12th, for distribution to the teachers, etc., of the First School District.

From the Minutes.

H. W. HALLIWELL,

Secretary.

Dignity and Importance of the Individual.

An Address to the Graduating Class, at the Commencement of the Central High School of Philadelphia, Thursday, February 12, 1885.

By ALBERT L. GIHON, A.M., M.D.

Of the Class of February, 1850.

Young Gentlemen of the Graduating Class :—

Among all the complimentary things that have happily fallen to my lot, nothing has gratified me more than the invitation to appear once again in the guise of a High School boy. Doubtless to you of the Eighty-third the Fifteenth Class seems far back in the misty past, and he a pretty old kind of boy who answers to its roll-call; yet to me it was only a short time since that I sat where you sit and fancied myself a hero—as I was and as you are—in the estimation of a fond mother and sister and admiring friends. The sounds of the music and applause; the perfume of the floral offerings; the glittering brightness of the gala morn; the blue-ribboned parchment, are now as they were then, and I might close my eyes and fancy I had merely closed a moment, and only dreamed I had lived these two score years and ten, but when I open them the mother and sister and devoted friend, who smiled with happy, tearful eyes upon me, are not here, and their absence makes me realize how wide and deep and dark is the gulf that lies between that yesterday and this to-day. To you the cloudland that fills this valley between the present and the future is bright with the sunlight of the opening day, and it is difficult for you to believe that, standing on the farther brink as I do, these same resplendent clouds can have a sombre side.

It were ungracious on an occasion like this to wail a dirge after your joyous pæans, and I would not for a moment check the exuberance of your joy by croaking harbingers of woe; but, perhaps, you will not think it amiss if an old school-fellow, who has jogged over life's highway a good half century, should point out to you the tree whose fruit is bitter, though it looks so fair, and warn you not to taste the ruddy apple that will turn to ashes on your lips.

Very likely you all consider this a veritable emancipation day, when you throw off the thrall of the master and are free to do your own will. Do not deceive yourselves. Life is one long servitude. Pleasure and happiness are the wages which labor brings. There are no seraph's wings to lift you without effort to heights beyond. The ascent must be gained toiling afoot over a rugged path, on which you will stumble and trip many times ere the summit be reached. I can give you no more earnest admonition than this, that nothing in this world can be done or gained without exertion, and that he who labors longest and most perseveringly will achieve most. Hence there is dignity and honor in work; ignominy and dishonor in idleness. The drone and laggard may seem to thrive at the expense of others, but they live as the parasite, and perish when they have no support to which to cling and on which to feed. Rich men's sons are so often distanced by the poor because the latter have had the spur of necessity to urge them in the race. Had you to-day your choice, certainly you would all ask your good fairy to give you the ten talents of moneyed capital, rather than the five of genius or the solitary one of a good education, but in the end you would find that capital without intelligence and culture would be wasted and bring you no return, and that the most gifted intellect, untrained and misdirected, would gather a scantier harvest than the patient plodding toiler who used his single talent as the studied experience of others had taught him it were wisest.

This, however, it is idle to expect you to fully recognize at this moment. If you have heedlessly spurned the gift of education, you will have only yourselves to blame, when at last you feel its want, and this will be when you jostle against other men in the rude encounters of life. The veneering of the sciolist rubs off at the first jar, and the sham is disclosed more plainly by the contrast. Little faults in language, unnoticed by their perpetrator, are indices of the uncultured man and woman, however stylishly or expensively arrayed. A single clink of the bogus coin betrays its base components ; a single misplaced point in writing, the one spoken solecism unconsciously parade the ignoramus. The asses' ears cannot be hidden under the borrowed skin.

Reverting for a moment to the studies of the past four years, which I hope none of you have neglected, or if you have skimmed them over that you will, by redoubled efforts before it is too late, regain the ground over which you have been distanced, you will recall how great a portion was devoted to the consideration of the wonderful objects in nature and the grand achievements of human art. Among all these wonders, has it occurred to you, that you are yourselves the most wonderful ? Have you ever reflected that this thing called man—this living, moving, speaking, thinking thing— is the most marvelous of all the created objects that we have ever seen or of which we can conceive ? Has not the fact that we are associated every moment of our lives with this creature, so accustomed us to its presence that we have never thought to imagine what it is, nor why it is ? Perhaps it is by reason of this long acquaintance that none of us have come to think any too well of this ever present familiar. Know thyself, the teacher cries, but see well, it is thy very self—that self which is nature's inimitable work. The glass pictures back form, face and lineaments—the outward semblance of a man, perhaps mis-shapen and of hideous mien, but for all, incomparable in the intricacy of its mechanism, and the mystery of its action. No human intellect has yet solved the problem of human existence. How a microscopic cell becomes a pretty infant, and how that little helpless creature grows to a robust man or lovely woman no one can tell. We only know that we exist, but do we ever reflect that in our individual existence is involved all other existence? This is the fact that I ask you to focus sharply before that mirror we call mind, that man—each man—you and I are not only creation's master-piece, but its all-comprehending end. All that has ever been done in this world, in the myriads upon myriads of years since it was formed from the nebulous floss of the eternal cosmos—all that the mind can conceive of other worlds and other existences—have been for you and me. You are the centre of the universe, and as knowledge carries you farther and farther into other realms, unlocks the mysteries of hidden truths, links you to the events of history, opening the gates to great wide fields of the unknown, that universe grows until it embraces all knowledge, and you are lord of all. Were you not, there were no Charlemagne, no Shakespeare, no Newton, no star-studded heavens, no broad expanse of ocean, no beautiful landscapes. The universe — this universe of yours — is bounded only by the horizon of your own knowledge. The rustic plough-boy, content to pass his life-time in the round of his humble occupation, lives in a world no larger than that of his four-footed companions of the kennel and the stable. The dolt, who eats and sleeps, and wakes to eat and sleep again, inhabits a dungeon shut out from the beauty and grandeur and sublimity of nature ; and self-imprisonment in cells as narrow and confined are they, who wear satin and broad-cloth and fine linen, but whose microcosms are as petty and inane as the boor's who is clad in home-spun, or the savage's scarce clad at all, the butterflies of fashion, the dudes and dudelets and dudines, who are only morbid excrescences on the social structure.

The measure of manhood, therefore, is the extent of each man's knowledge. The more varied and profound his acquirements, the wider his acquaintance with the uttermost parts of the world in which he dwells, the farther he is able to peer into the past and future, and to scan what is all around him, the loftier will be the throne he occupies, the greater the multitudes who owe him allegiance. Each one of you is monarch of all he surveys, and his kingdom .the greatest who daily adds new conquests to his possessions. He who speaks two languages is twice a man, for a new people is added to his realm ; his wealth

the greater, who gathers new treasures within the storehouse of
his mind. He lives best who learns most, and does not fritter
away his days on the rounds of the treadmill.

Who would explore the maze of nature's labyrinth, must
bear in mind that this is not idle play. Its many chambered
temples can only be visited by groping in the dark in search of
their hidden entrances. The task is great and the days are few;
hence, he who would accomplish much, must remember Frank-
lin's admonishment "Dost thou love life? then do not squander
time for that's the stuff life is made of." "Let every man be
master of his time," says Shakespeare, for "Time is an estate
that will produce nothing without culture, but will abundantly
repay the labors of industry." (Johnson.) If life is worth living,
then husband every hour, that the sum of your enjoyment may
be so much the greater. Centuries are made up of minutes,
and history is only the aggregate of the thoughts and deeds of
the moment. The wasted hour shortens the span of our existence and is irrevocably lost.

Yet after all this mighty monarch, whose rule is so bound-
less, and whose subjects are all the living and the dead, is nothing but a mere machine—a mechanism of flesh and blood and
bone and sinew—most intricately interlaced—but still only an
aggregate of organs and apparatus, which it is your especial
charge—each one of you—to care for—to beautify—improve—
develop—and perfect to the fullest possible extent—and this is
the one especial point I have had prominently in view in address-
ing you to day. I doubt whether any of your instructors have
sufficiently inculcated upon you this lesson, which is so import-
ant for you to take to heart, which you will neglect to your ir-
reparable injury, and can never after remedy by any repentant
industry—the prime importance of the care of health. If some
other order of being could look upon this earth and see us as we
are—discern that all our conscious interests are involved in this
physical existence—that our being depends upon the maintenance
of the activity of its organic elements and our pleasures upon
their harmonious play—that being could not possibly conceive

that we, possessing intellects ourselves, to know these things, could be so indifferent to them. When death is near, good and bad alike shrink at his approach. The shipwrecked mariner slays his shipmate, and the parent sacrifices his child for a few hours longer sorrow—but when the shadow of the wings of the dark angel does not chill us, we are blind and deaf and senseless, living as the fool lives and treading where angels would not dare. Braggarts when there is no enemy of pestilence or disease we are arrant cowards and cry lustily enough—" Help me, ere I sink "—when it is too late.

Nor is it only the ignorant who are so heedless. The erudite philosopher is apt to be the gravest sanitary sinner, and old men, who have but a few more beads upon their rosary to tell, handle their chaplet as unconcernedly as the youth—nevertheless, the folly of the wise should not deter me from impressing upon you that if you would govern well this great kingdom of which you are the ruler, you must first strive to make yourselves fit to rule. Puny, feeble and sickly you will be impotent for good ; lusty, vigorous and healthy, strong-minded, clear-eyed and bright-minded, you will be that man whose dominion is over every living thing that moveth upon the earth. The *mens sana* dwells only *in corpore sano*. The windows of the senses, through which the soul looks upon the outside world, must be wide opened to let in the full flood of light and harmony—not be half closed by disease, nor shaded by physical defects. To think well one must have no clouded brain—to feel well no broken circuit of nerve power. The blood must course briskly and unobstructed through every tiny vessel ; it must be washed clean of effete matters in the air bath of the lungs. The waste which follows action must be repaired by new and better material, which only a sound digestive apparatus prepares, assimilates and vivifies. If we have had a grimy hirsute ancestor, he who has the whitest, softest skin may claim to be the most remote of kin. We grow in god-like-ness as we cultivate the graces of the body—and the chief of these is cleanliness.

Perhaps I have not stated my meaning in terms sufficiently explicit and emphatic. Recognizing man as the *summum bonum* of animated existence, this man must be the worthiest object of his own study and care. Incomparable among created things, formed in the image and after the likeness of divinity, endowed with self-consciousness and thought, deified as the seat of the living soul, human forethought can scarce be too great for the preservation of this wondrous mechanism, which makes him what he is. A little patch upon the brain transforms the genius into a driveling idiot; a little spot upon the eye shuts out all the glories of his surroundings; a little break in the spinal cord binds him fast as Prometheus to the rock. Over all the avenues to wrong-doing the command is written, Thou shalt not! There is a monitor within who speaks loudly enough if we will but listen, who warns us whither we should not go. The right path is always bright and he only loses his way who plunges into obscure thickets, whence the road can only be retraced with loss of time. The giddy girl courts pleasure at untimely hours and pays the penalty in suffering and sorrow, for nature is a usurer who exacts exorbitant interest for borrowed capital. The pound of flesh must be repaid though it be cut from the very heart, and the children and the children's children of the spendthrift of his health are left a heritage of debt. Not only is disease, which is the visible evidence of bodily disorder, the effect of sanitary mis-doing, but crime, the mental and moral manifestation of maladies no less physical, likewise traces its inception to the violation of the laws of health. The morbid brain hatches mischief—the dyspeptic stomach colors the imaginings with lurid hues and incites to deeds of darkness. The pang of pain extorts a curse or cry of rage. Sordid and meretricious writings, the frenzies of fanatics, all the abominable offenses against social law and order, the demoniac doings of them possessed with devils begin with some poison in the blood—some thorn in the flesh of the evil-doer or his progenitors.

The effects of the neglect of health are so momentous that the care of the body is therefore one of our most serious obligations, and it cannot be alleged that that is ignoble which has so high an aim on the one hand or on the other such disastrous consequences. Consider it your first duty to take care of your bodies—to keep them clean, to nurture them, develop, strengthen, improve and beautify them. Live as much as possible in the open air, because without air you cannot live at all. Seek the bright light of heaven, because light is the most powerful animating influence. Exercise every organ, because action is the essence of life, and the unused muscle, brain or sense withers and becomes useless. If you take abundant exercise in the sunshine and fresh air, you will require no bolstering potions to make you sleep, no iron to give you vigor, no appetizing cordial to tempt you to eat, drink and be merry. By exercise I do not mean a circus performance with dumb bells, Indian clubs and iron balls, nor by bathing a shivering amphibious existence in a tub of cold water—not the extravagant athletics of the gymnasium and racing boat, but such a rational, temperate activity of body as will give every organ that healthful performance of its functions which is necessary for its normal growth and development. The life of each ultimate component cell is an epitome of that of the aggregated mass of cells which forms a human body. It is born, it grows, performs its alloted act and dies, leaving another like it —better than it if it have done its part well; degenerate, ill-conditioned, fecund of evil if it have not thrived. Strive, therefore, to attain the soundest physical condition possible, but do not mistake that muscle only is man, else the professional bruiser would be paragon of men; nor yet be deluded by that caricature of manhood, the empty fop, whose peacock body is glossed with cosmetics and tricked with fashion's fine feathers. A healthy man is one who can do well all that doth become a man—nor more, nor less.

There are many who, racked by pain and enfeebled by disease, succeed where others fail, but they are like the armless woman who has learned to sew with her toes, or the deaf mute who has been taught to read the play of your lips and utter sounds he cannot hear. The energy wasted in their patient

triumph over such obstacles would have made them heroes had
their lots been different. For your own sakes, therefore, if only
for the selfish end that your sense of pleasure may be more keen,
your capacity for enjoyment greater, be mindful of yourselves;
and if your ambition be the nobler one of making others happy,　•
the outspoken joyousness of your own exuberant well-being,
like ripples on the placid surface of the water, will spread in
ever widening circles all around you.

I will have done enough if I can succeed in impressing
upon you the consciousness of your own nobility; the dignity
and importance of your own body; the obligations imposed upon
you to care for that body without ceasing—first, as individuals,
for the sake of the personal gratification you will derive; second,
as sons and brothers and husbands and fathers, on account of the
happiness it will bring to those who hold you dear, and whose
comfort and support may depend upon the strength of your
right arm; third, as members of society, for the good you will
accomplish for your fellow-men by giving thought to the preservation of health—the health of yourselves and that of your
neighbors. At this very time there is a general awakening of
interest in questions of public health. The slow but sure
approach of a dreaded epidemic has aroused communities to the
question of self-protection, but all precautionary measures ulti-
mately resolve themselves into the elements of personal hygiene.
The health of the community is only the aggregate of the sanitary condition of its individual members, and it becomes the
duty of every man, woman and child to contribute his, her and
its share to the public weal. Here the child is greater than his
sire. The pliant, undeveloped structure can be trained to grow
well-formed and stately; the oak gnarled by age and exposure
must bear its knots to the end; but you can prune and train and
culture yourselves into both strength and comeliness. The
lessons in hygiene may have fallen idly on your ears, but here-
after, not as a compulsory task, but as an entertaining pastime,　•
I beg you to recall these lessons and give them serious heed.

Health is the foundation of success, but it only enables the work of life to be well done. It lightens the burthen, but the task must still be performed. It is coadjutor to industry, zeal, ambition, determination, and when misfortune comes, it is the raft which bears the shipwrecked mariner back to port, for the fairest day may become o'er clouded. Often without premonition, the wind veers and the sail is taken aback, but the skilful navigator instead of folding his hands and crying. "God's will be done," trims his sails and steers another course. Richelieu's aphorism that "in the bright lexicon of youth there's no such word as fail" does not apply to special enterprises. Disappointment and disaster like the falling rain drop upon good and bad alike, but the man determined to prosper casts aside the soiled garments and betakes himself anew to his task.

Only one misfortune will befall you, which you will find hard to meet resignedly, however fortified by reason, religion or philosophy—the loss of those who love you and who are loved by you. You do not realize how largely in the exultation of to-day enter the glad smiles of a mother, a sister or a dear friend. Only when the mother lies cold and speechless—when the pure spirit of your sister has taken its flight to a better sphere and all that is left of her on earth rests beneath the mound on which bloom flowers that are less pure than she, will you know what real sorrow means?

I will not detain you further, nor drag out the last long hour of weary waiting for the word *Go*, to start upon the race for fame and fortune. I have sought to make you understand that the universe in which you exist is as large and great as you choose to make it ; that you, who are its centre, will yourself be great and grand, petty and insignificant as you elect, that the price you pay for the boon of living is toil, and that he only reaps who sows, and he only garners good grain who sows good seed.

In northern climes the days lengthen out their hours of sunshine, and as the year advances these gradually lessen until they are overwhelmed in the day-long night. Thus with our lives. In the beginning, time seems to move all too slowly, the long bright days almost merging into one. Then is the season for ceaseless activity. Linger though we may upon the scene, the latter will always be the shorter half of our lives, and we should so act, therefore, that when the twilight comes, we may rest content that we have toiled well and have no bitter regrets for wasted golden hours. May you all be able to look back upon your class-mates of to-day, as I can upon mine, recalling only pleasant memories. We parted friends, and those of us who survive are friends to-day. May you too, a generation hence, be able to indulge in just such retrospections. Especially, may you feel the same pride that we, its alumni, who now welcome you among their number, do in the noble institution, which is our honored *Alma Mater.*